CW01499423

Girl
Good Enough

and further raw poems on
girlhood, womanhood, love, life and death

Annie Lloyd-Hyde

Illustrations by Fran Rawlings

First published 2022 by Compass Publishing

ISBN - 978-1-913713-74-4

Copyright © Annie Lloyd-Hyde, 2022

Illustration and artwork © Fran Rawlings Art, 2022

Edited and typeset by A Neater Page

The right of Annie Lloyd-Hyde to be identified as the author of this work has been asserted in accordance with the Copyright, Designs and Patents Act, 1988. All rights reserved. No part of this publication may be reproduced, stored in a retrieval system, or transmitted, in any form or by any means (electronic, mechanical, photocopying, recording or otherwise), without the prior written permission of the publisher. This book is a work of fiction. Names, characters, places and incidents are either a product of the author's imagination or are used fictitiously. Any resemblance to actual people living or dead, events or locales is entirely coincidental.

A CIP catalogue record for this book is available from the British Library

Printed and bound by Ecclesall Print, Sheffield, England

Contact: anne.yeadonpoetry@gmail.com

Foreword

For all the Daves

Contents

Good Girl Syndrome

Beware the Good Girl syndrome

Once caught

It's hard to cure

Needing approval

Confirmation of worth

The need for perfection

Excessive

A curse.

React

Resist

Play a wider game

Think beyond the box,

Mistakes can be worthy

Revealing

Creative

Could lead to solutions

You might never have found

When you were a Good Girl

With your nose to the ground.

So, kick the Good Girl well into touch

Leave that perfection stuff

Metamorphose, revitalise, grow

Become

Girl – Good Enough.

Memories of Childhood Summers

We are powered by perpetual sunshine
We have all the time in the world
Cycling fast, cycling free
Country lanes
Endless skies.

The rhythm of our pedals
Matches the rhythm of our thoughts
We are on automatic
We are away with our dreams
Meditation on wheels.

Lincolnshire
Offering no resistance
To our spinning summer legs
We are in a recurring loop
Sunshine, freedom, time.

Best friends and best laid plans
And we *may* carry them out
We drink from our bottles
And gaze across fields
At rows of regimented crops.

We live in the moment
Nettles and dock leaves
Lurid sweets in white paper bags
Sworn secrets
And a skylark's song.

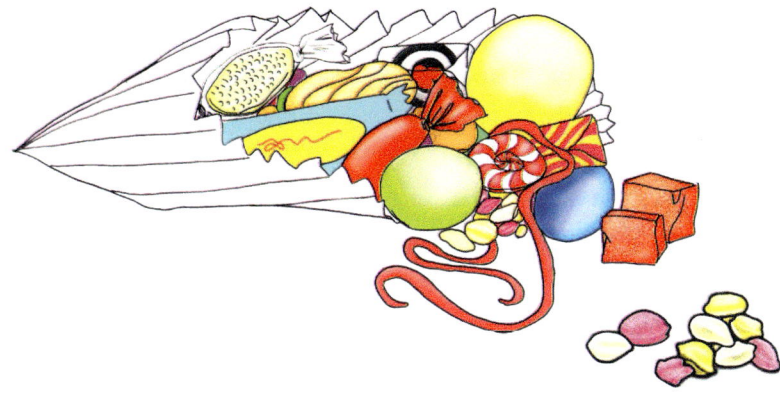

My Plumber Poet

Some girls dream of marrying a prince
Or some other handsome stunner
But I've long harboured a secret desire
For a poetry writing plumber.

I'd have a home that's water tight
And a home that's warm with words
With my boiler well-adjusted
As my radiators purr.

And my poetry writing plumber
Has me for his muse
With mixer taps in second place
I'm plunged into beatitude.

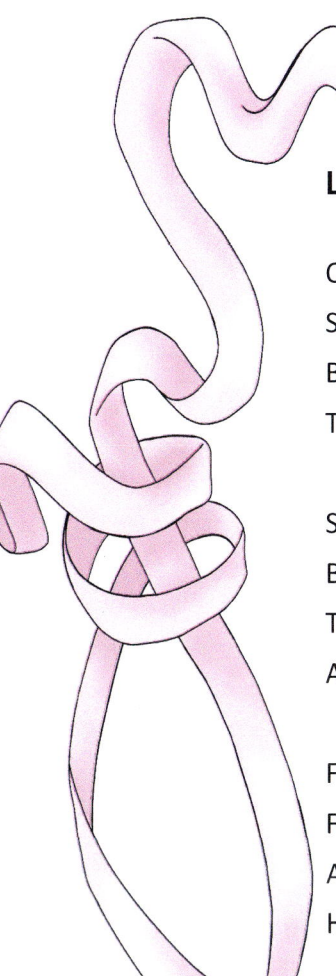

Loneliness

On Saturday the world held a party
She wasn't invited to go
But she heard the sounds of revelry
The music, the laughter below.

She shut the windows, pulled the blinds
But not before she saw
That all the world had turned up
And was dancing round her door.

For them, food and wine and friendship
For her, the bereavement of hope
A confirmation of her worthlessness
Her world at the end of a rope.

Flirtation

Was this, she wondered, flirtation
Or was it more of a flurry
An awareness of feeling something
Elusive, unsure, blurry.

Was a smile, she wondered, flirtation
Or just friendly, everyday stuff
If it had a touch of a linger
Does that qualify, is it enough?

A glance could be flirtation
If it lasted to a count of three
Size of pupils could indicate something
But she's not near enough to see.

And so these thoughts continue to run
Like Hamlet's soliloquy
To see, or not to see, flirtation
Or oppose such frivolity.

Dog-Share

It started with a dog-share
Then things sort of moved on
And now we've got a man-share
And we're having much more fun.

We have him on alternate days
He keeps us in the loop
Sunday is his day of rest
And we relax, re-group.

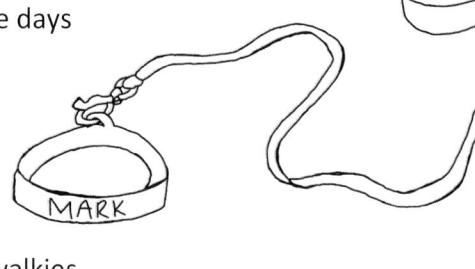

With him, I'm free from walkies
Though I'm sure he could ably fetch
And so it's working really well
At least no problems I can detect.

His screwdriver skills are impeccable
His curries are simply divine
I don't need to keep any treats to hand
He obeys and sits first time.

My man-sharer's really happy
Says it gives her a 'relationship break'
Puts romance back into their marriage
And she knows where he is if he's late.

The List

1. Write a list

- An essential ritual
- Satisfying
- Gratifying
- Addictive
- Habitual
- Fulfilling
- A need
- For order
- Control
- For an item ticked
- Is an item that's flown
- Lightening the soul

Pip List

My mother had a 'Pip List'
Like the Oscars in reverse
Where those who had annoyed her
Were unveiled.
No awards or ego trips
Just "Oh, he gets on my pip!" and
WHOOSH
Another victim was nailed.
So, they were …
    The Know-it-alls
    The Have-it-alls
    The Over-confident
    The Chirpy
    The Overdressed
    The Underdressed
    The Tattooed
    The Quirky
    The Pierced
    The Dyed
    The Wealthy
    And The Mean.
Oh, and finally, those
    Near-naked
    Lusting on the screen.

How to Be

My mother held me
When I was born
She cradled me
Loved unconditionally
Taught me how to be
And whichever road I travelled
Foolish or wise
She unravelled me
And we smiled.

I held my mother
As she died
I held her tight
I cradled her
For she had shown me how to be
And this last road she travelled
Was away from me
And her beating heart was still
And I could weep.

Walking Home Alone

Missing
But we dared to hope
Missing
We held our breath
A young woman
Smiling out a trust in the world.

Fatal timing
Fatal meeting
A minute sooner?
A second later?
But it was not meant to be
For a force of good, a force of love
Met a force of dark inhumanity.

Her innocence is sacrificed
Darkened trees echo the mood
There's an uneasy re-awakening
Of a woman's vulnerability
Her perpetual culpability
For simply
Being a woman
Walking home.

In dedication to Sarah Everard, Nicole Smallman and Bibaa Henry

The Crazed Protector of You

As you were born
So I was born
With a powerful urge to protect
Overwhelming, all engulfing
Out-of-the-blue perplexed.
Dark, shadowed emotions
Flooded my soul
Irrevocably, unwaveringly
Transforming my role
Into the Crazed Protector of you.

You – out in the world?
My doubt in the world
A walk in the park?
It's approaching dark
Busy street?
What if we meet …
A racing car, a drug-fuelled youth
An angry dog, a tiger (loose)
For I am the Crazed Protector of you.

And when you are older
And I am wiser
And you are busy
And I'm content
I will still be there for you
Ever vigilant, ever true
Always the Crazed Protector
The Crazed Protector of you.

My Name

Was it a lack of imagination
Or simply chagrin
That caused my parents
To call me Anne.

Maybe a weariness
As the third daughter born
That hindered creativity
In the eye of a post-natal storm.

Annie, Anna, Annabel
They would have been just fine
But being an indefinite article
Can sometimes undermine.

Quirks

I must stop collecting
My mother's quirks
I have enough of my own.
Nature allotted me my share
So nurture should leave me alone.

Panic Attack

My orchestral panic attack
My loud beating heart
Feel like I'm tuning up
And this is just the start.

I'm all discordant
I'm all out of tune
Rhythmic breathing shallow
Breaths coming too soon.

Too forte, too allegro
On an adrenaline high
Heading for a crescendo
Fear I'm going to die.

Need everything to slow
Need harmony and calm
Cadence, silence, inner peace
A soothing, calming balm.

Doors

When I lose myself in dreams
There's a corridor I visit
Lined with doors cast in shadows
I'm alone.
The doors are from the past
Forgotten, unfamiliar
Then a sudden realisation and I know

The front door in my childhood
The handle just too high,
The bedroom door that locked
In Pear Tree Lane,
The creaking pantry door
In my grandma's busy kitchen,
The kaleidoscope of memories still remain.

When I venture through a door
The kaleidoscope is clearer
And I free-fall into warm familiarity.
I see my life and its pathways
In my myriad of dreams
I see the choices that I made
These other versions of me.

I Wish

I wish I was a statistic
Then you might caress me
Finger my variables
With sensuous desire

I'd deal with your data
Sooner, not later
And you'd realise my procedures
Were appetisingly secure

Don't wish to be big-headed
But my methodology? Legendary!
With deviations and anomalies
Swiftly sorted and with ease.

My control group's appropriate
Representative too
Couldn't abide any miscreants
Unless the deviant was you!

And when you read my conclusions
You'll be impressed at first sight
You'll be falling at my feet
In pure statistical delight.

To Trust or Not to Trust

Dare she trust again?
    It's a gamble
    Dare she go back, re-join the dance?
    Post betrayal scars are fading
    Images, memories, less pervading
    Less ram-raiding of her mind.
    But, in her heart she's not intact.

Suspicion
    Takes such energy
    Such watchfulness, such negativity
    That drains the heart, darkens the soul
    It's wearying, trust on parole.

So, she'll re-join the dance
    She'll take the leap
    Let the consequences fly
    Presume redemption – a new sensation
    And her head will be held high.

I Am Your Wayward Heart

Long-term memory
Short-term memory
Muscle memory
Then me
I am your heartbeat memory
I am your wayward heart
Unabashed by rule and reason
Where logic plays no part.

So, if HE should walk into the room
You can be assured
I will instantly remember
I will instantly recall.
With signals switched to red alert
You'll feel the instant hit
A hot wave of confusion
Causing you to submit
All reason.

For your mouth will be desert dry

Your stomach will be fluttering

Your conversation limited

Just incoherent muttering

And the urge to flee, compelling

With your wayward heart dispelling

Any sense.

Long-term memory

Short-term memory

Muscle memory

Then me

I am your heartbeat memory

I am your wayward heart.

Pain

Pain is hopeless at telling the time
Doesn't get 'moving on'
Will cling to each moment
Keep you constrained
When really he should have long gone.

Pain says his leaving is imminent
Or very soon after that
But vulnerability's compelling
There's really no telling
When you'll be freed from his grasp.

Now I've accepted that pain's here to stay
I've shifted to give him more room
For it's simply less wearying
Than perpetual railing
To have him inside my cocoon.

Funeral for the Earth

The funeral for the earth
Was a quiet affair
Shrouded in mist
And despondency
No consolatory words
To soothe or placate
No creature present
For them all too late
Just the souls of the dead
The spirit of trees
Memories of past times
But who would believe?
Only the angels
Smudges of light
Floating, free in the emptiness
Searching into the night.

Neversayno

Neversayno

In the state of **Perfectionville**

Found high in the clouds

Five miles east of **Impossible**.

The journey is long

But it has to be made

Facing wearisome challenges

So you find your Brave.

You make it

And it's worth it

There's a job at **Toomuchville**!

It's yours and you're told

You can start straight away.

Most tasks take infinity

A challenge it's true

Perfection in all things

But demanded by who?

You're organised, you're willing

You're *so* eager to please

But, despite all your efforts

At promotion, you're squeezed

By the young, the dark-suited

The entitled and cool

Who rise up the ranks

With the Connections Rule.

And you, disconnected

Unentitled, unsuited

Remain downstairs

Your worth diluted.

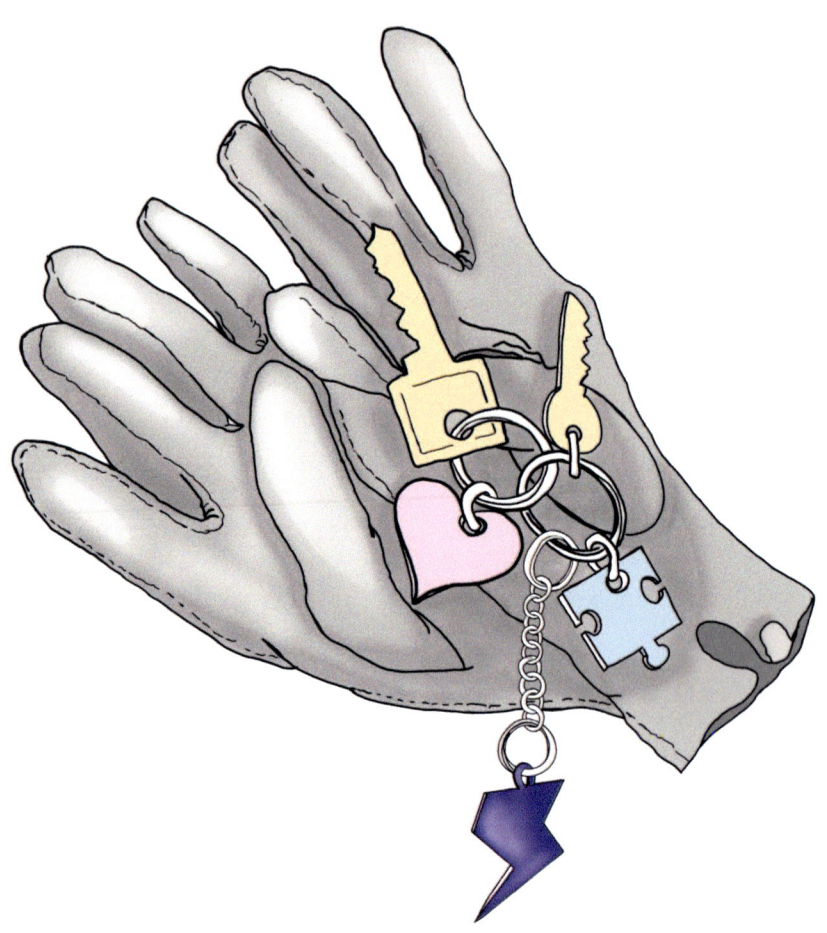

The Glove

You're the glove that fits my hand
You're the jigsaw piece that's missing
You're the one with the key to my heart
You're my better late than never
You're the one who's mine forever
Haunting my dreams
Right from the start.

You're the one who I would follow
To the ends of the earth
Our martinis always shaken, not stirred
You are the apple of my eye
You're my derring-do or die
Each moment seized
And you're the reason why.

I know I could say more
But I fear I could be sinking
In a boat of cliched thinking
Little hope of survival
Unless a chance arrival
Of a bolt out of the blue,
Delivering the one and only
Never to be forgotten
You.

Free-falling

I am *free-falling* into my mother

An observation, not a critique
I'm assuming some of her stances
Her whims and ways and fancies
Her irreverence.

Hills lifted mother's spirits
As did her gang of mates
She had a sound sense of the silly
Wrote mad verse for them on key dates.

We talk in dreams, my mother and I,
I thank her for all she gave me
A love of words, a sense of fun
And simply exquisite gravy.

Rough and Ready Poetry

Rough and ready poetry
Ricocheted from the heart
From where you keep your fragile fears
Your secret dreams
Your art.
And when your poetry ripens
Try it on for size
Take your words through their paces
And when they've earned their places
Light the blue touchpaper
And retreat.

Rage, Rage Against the Dying of the World

Angry planet

Apocalyptic world

Taking up arms

Against a sea of indifference

Spinning between

Crazed extremes

And we are dizzy.

Does some

Unseen judge

Watch the turmoil

The over-powering heat

The rising floods

And think

"They should have known".

Now we watch

Now we listen

Now we know it's here

Now we race against

The dying of the day

Now we rage, rage against

The dying of the world

With thanks to Dylan Thomas

Notes

Example: How good are you?